Preaching Old Testament Narrative

Bob Fyall

Tutor in Biblical Studies (Old Testament),
Cranmer Hall, St John's College, Durham

Minister of Claypath United Reformed Church

GROVE BOOKS LIMITED
RIDLEY HALL RD CAMBRIDGE CB3 9HU

Contents

Foreword

This booklet aims to explore the fascination of Old Testament narrative and to help people to teach and preach this more effectively. This is a vast subject and raises numerous issues which deserve fuller consideration. If it stimulates people to love the Bible more and to preach it more effectively as well as to explore the issues further then it will have fulfilled its purpose.

Much of this material has already been presented orally in a series of sermons preached in Claypath United Reformed Church in Durham in Autumn 1994 and in an Adult Education Class in St John's College, Durham in early 1996.

I would like to thank the Grove Biblical group for their invitation to write this booklet.

The Cover Illustration is by Peter Ashton

First Impression June 1997
ISSN 1365-490X
ISBN 1 85174 346 4

1
Telling the Story

'So we are just like David,' said the preacher, 'we need to kill the giants in our lives. We have to use the stones. Bible study, prayer, worship, quiet times and outreach.' That or similar statements are not untypical of many sermons on biblical narrative. The assumption is that we can jump immediately to application, and in this particular case that we can identify ourselves with David. This booklet will attempt to suggest and demonstrate ways in which we can more seriously engage with the text and thus more effectively communicate its message.

It is vital to establish right away the importance of careful listening to the text and of seeing how it fits into the larger picture. This booklet is not simply about understanding and preaching individual Bible stories but about seeing how this must be controlled by reference to the larger story. In the David story, for example, David is not simply an individual, he is already the Lord's anointed and as such symbolizes God's champion who comes against Goliath 'in the name of the Lord of hosts, the God of the armies of Israel' (1 Samuel 17.45). When we look at the wider picture, we are much more like the terrified Israelites cowering helplessly until, to paraphrase Newman, 'a second David to the fight and to the rescue came.'

In the booklet, 1 and 2 Kings will be used as a case study to illustrate some of the general principles underlying preaching from biblical narrative.[1] This chapter will look at more general issues such as why concentrate on narrative and the way in which story and theology relate.

The Importance of Story

Story is important in the Bible not least because there is much of it. In our English Bibles there are two major blocks of narrative, Genesis to 2 Kings and 1 Chronicles to Esther, which both tell the story from creation to exile and its immediate aftermath. In the prophets, there is a lot of biographical and historical material especially in Jeremiah and even in the Wisdom books and the Psalter there is a fair amount of narrative—for example, the story of Job and Psalms such as 78 which summarize the history of Israel. In the New Testament the heart of the message is the events surrounding the life, death and resurrection of Jesus and the life of the early church flowing from these.

From this it is clear that the Bible presents a more-or-less coherent story

---

[1]   My brief for this booklet was *Old Testament* narrative but much of what is said would, I believe, be valid for the gospels and Acts.

or plot line from creation to consummation. When we plunge into any part of that great story or 'metanarrative'(to use current jargon) we will need to see how individual stories fit into the broad picture. The main moves of the plot—creation, fall, call of Abraham, exodus, settlement, exile, incarnation, cross, resurrection, Pentecost and coming and new creation—must be firmly grasped. This will prevent us taking individual stories and making them mean what they cannot mean, whilst at the same time each individual story will both depend on and strengthen our understanding and appreciation of the larger story.

We cannot, therefore, do anything like justice to preaching on the Bible unless we handle narrative.

Story and Theology

'Story' is the flavour of the month in much contemporary theology. Books have multiplied on narrative theology; papers and conferences devoted to 'telling our stories' have proliferated. The didactic form of sermon has increasingly been seen as static and wedded to an abstract view of truth, working well if the passage itself is didactic (as with the New Testament letters) but wholly inappropriate for narrative. Thus the narrative form is held to be more appropriate for those vast areas of the Bible which tell a story.

The advantages of a sermon which is itself in story form are obvious enough. The first is the great involvement of the listeners' emotions and imagination as well as their minds. Preachers help the listeners to enter the world of the story and into more participation with it. Also, it works indirectly and thus obviates hostility to the message. However, while arguing that literary genres are a vital part of understanding, this booklet is not advocating a story-telling approach to the preaching of biblical narrative. In particular there are three criticisms I have of over-reliance on the story-telling form.

The first pitfall is doing badly what the Bible does well. In place of a memorable, vivid narrative we can end up with a limp paraphrase. There is a place for a vivid recreation of a narrative as part of a sermon, a point to which I shall return. Similarly, well-told stories, especially those which emphasize the plot line of the Bible, are important in teaching children.[2]

A second pitfall is the danger of suggesting that we are dealing with a *potpourri* of unconnected stories with a tenuous or non-existent connection with historical truth. If the Bible's plot line is a record of the activities in God in time and space (and beyond) we must expect a basic coherence and factuality. This is not to argue that historical truth is the only kind of truth which

---

2   One of the best such books is *The Children's Bible in 365 Stories* by Mary Batchelor (Lion, 1985).

matters in biblical narrative. But I do believe that for an event to be theologically interpreted it must first have happened.[3]

A third pitfall is to imagine that the point has been made when all that has happened is that the story has been enjoyed. Even the fact that the listeners' emotions have been touched does not in itself mean that the point has been grasped. David was deeply moved by Nathan's story but completely failed to grasp its application until told 'you are the man' (2 Samuel 12.7).

Story and Preaching

Most of us love stories. We read the stories of David and Goliath, Daniel in the lion's den or Paul's shipwreck and are moved and excited. How do we convey something of that when we are preaching? I believe that we must begin by asking what it is in stories which fascinates us. Before looking at a specific biblical example (the books of 1 and 2 Kings which are a good example of sustained historical narrative), we shall try to ask what aspects of story we should study and try to bring out in our preaching.

We must first look at *plot*, the actual sequence of events which almost always introduces a conflict and its complications. The two stories I look at illustrate two different kinds of plot. The Solomon story (1 Kings 1-11) is leisurely and full of description, especially of the building of the temple. It is the preacher's task to show how event and comment subtly blend together and by placing Solomon in the great story of God's purposes help the listeners to relate their own stories to this.

The other story (2 Kings 18-19) is one of nail-biting suspense. It moves swiftly and powerfully and the dramatic nature of the outcome and the huge issues that depend on it make this a gripping narrative. It is important to work hard on background so that the scene can be imagined and its essence communicated.

The plot is the dynamic which drives the story as a whole. It is the biblical text itself which has the power; the preacher's task is to help people to reflect on how plot contributes to the total impact of the story and thus how that part of Scripture can most effectively be understood.

But we must also look at *characterization*, the kind of people we are reading about. We have no description of 'Solomon, in all his glory,' and although we know David is handsome, that is a very general description. This does not mean, however, that they are flat characters. The character of Solomon is a complex one and I try in chapter 3 to bring this out in tracing his decline from magnificence to ineffectiveness.

---

3 Some argue that historicity in the parables of Jesus is unimportant—for example, we do not know the name of the good Samaritan or the sower or even if they refer to specific incidents or are 'true to life stories.' But such details are not part of the Bible's plot line of events but illustrations of them.

What is also significant is the way that 'typical' characters recur. For example Elijah is the new Moses, denouncing Ahab as Moses had Pharaoh, challenging the priests of Baal as Moses had the magicians of Pharaoh, and meeting God at the holy mountain. Hezekiah, as we shall see in chapter 4, is the new David standing up to the Assyrian Goliath. This is one of the important ways in which each character gains significance from the whole plot line of the Bible and leads us to Christ.

A question to ask of story in addition to 'what' (plot) and 'who' (characterization) is 'where' (*setting*). On one level this is fairly simple. A fundamental aid for understanding biblical narrative is a good atlas. The story of Hezekiah and Sennacherib (2 Kings 18 and 19) becomes much clearer when the setting of the events is examined. The route followed by the Assyrians as they come to attack Jerusalem takes them across the valley of Elah where, of course, the apparently helpless David had destroyed Goliath. These hills and valleys had already been and would be again the scene of God's saving acts.

A fourth question to ask of these stories is 'how' (*point of view*). No story can ever be neutral and the stance of the author and the manner in which the story is told is an important factor in listening to what the story is saying to us. There is first the point of view of the narrator who assesses the various kings in terms of whether they did or did not do 'what was right in the eyes of the Lord' (2 Kings 12.2, 13.2, 11 and so on). But this is not done by simply chronicling a series of events. We see how the different characters also dramatize points of view. In 1 Kings 22 we have a vivid evocation of the scene from three perspectives. We have the establishment view from Ahab and his prophets, the uncertain and confused view of Jehoshaphat and the prophetic view of Micaiah which the outcome of the story makes clear is the narrator's own view.

These are the theoretical principles which underlie what is illustrated in chapters 2-4 of the booklet. Once we have understood the text clearly and invited the listeners to enter the world of biblical narrative then our task is to apply it and following the specific examples in chapters 2-4 we shall explore more fully in chapter 5 how this might be done.

2
How Shall We Begin?

In his novel *Witchwood*, John Buchan tells of an ancient minister who preached for eighty two weeks on Exodus 15.27. This text tells of how the escaping Israelites came to Elim with its twelve springs and seventy palm trees. 'Worthy Mr McMichael took a week to each well and a week to each palm tree.'[4] This little anecdote encapsulates some of the suspicions many people feel about expository preaching. The first is that this kind of preaching simply plods through the text with mind-numbing tedium. The second is that, particularly in the Old Testament, the passage becomes a springboard for the preacher's speculations. In the biblical text, nothing whatever is made of the fact that Elim had wells and palm trees apart from the obvious point that it was a useful oasis for the people to rest and was a contrast with Marah and the bitter water of the previous verses.

Plainly, as we move now to consider 1 and 2 Kings as a case-study we want to avoid both the dull recounting of plot or the extracting of propositions which were identified in chapter 1 as the main dangers of preaching on biblical narrative. We will do this best, I believe, by pausing for a moment to consider the books as a whole. I shall then outline a plan for a series of ten studies on the book and discuss the principles of selection.

The two books are a unity, the story running continuously from the dying days of David to the Exile. It has, of course, many links with the earlier part of the story in Genesis to Samuel as well as anticipating the story still to come. However, by trying to understand Kings we shall be in a better position to look at biblical narrative as a whole. Three particular issues will help us to focus this.

Kings sets out to tell a story. Passages such as 1 Kings 6 and 7 describe the temple, but on the whole the narrative flows with a wealth of incident and character. We will need to trace the thread and the unifying themes and have respect for the artistry and coherence of the book. So an inescapable foundation for preaching the book will be repeated reading until the flow and structure become clear.

Secondly, historical issues, while not obtrusive, must figure in our understanding of the text. Kings is concerned to show us how the covenant community of ancient Israel tried and failed to live in the promised land. Good

---

4   See *Witchwood* by John Buchan (Edinburgh, 1988) p 9.

7

historical writing will share many of the qualities of all good narrative.[5]

Thirdly (and this is relevant to how we preach it) Kings is history from a theological perspective. This means we have to be aware of those themes given greatest importance in the book. The supremacy of the God of Israel is crucial both in worship and living. The place of the prophetic word and the divine perspective on history will be emphasized again and again. The reasons leading to the exile will be presented and the involvement of God in national and international affairs woven into the texture of the narrative. Good history not only recounts the past but interprets it and its significance for the present. It is not an attempt to tell everything and it organizes time and events into sizable units.

The thinking behind this booklet is not simply that we must preach Bible stories but that the sweep of biblical narrative needs to be tackled as well. Having read and reread Kings and grasped the main sequence of the narrative, our next task is to work out an outline of studies which will try to draw attention to the highlights of the book as a whole. The following outline is a series of ten sermons I preached between October and December 1994. The series was entitled 'Our God Reigns: Sweeping through 1st and 2nd Kings.'

1. Half-hearted commitment—the tragedy of Solomon (1 Kings 1-11).
2. Two ways of getting it wrong—Rehoboam and Jeroboam (1 Kings 12-14).
3. The God who answers by fire—Elijah and the prophets of Baal (1 Kings 18).
4. Whose land is it anyway?—Naboth's vineyard (1 Kings 21).
5. I saw the Lord—Micaiah's vision (1 Kings 22).
6. But he was a leper—The story of Naaman (2 Kings 5).
7. Joash tries to put it right (2 Kings 12).
8. The Lord enthroned in Zion. Hezekiah's miraculous escape (2 Kings 18 and 19).
9. David comes again—Josiah's reformation (2 Kings 22 and 23).
10. O come, O come Immanuel. Exile and beyond (2 Kings 25).

What were the principles of selection behind these ten studies? The overall aim was, as always, to build up people's faith and present the gospel to unbelievers. In this series I wanted to create an excitement for biblical stories, and so encourage the congregation to read the text for themselves. This is more likely to happen if people have some landmarks to guide them as they plunge in and try to navigate their way through this bewildering ocean of material.

---

5 Whether a story is history or fiction cannot be determined on stylistic criteria. The fact that a story is well written simply shows that it is the work of a good writer not that it is fiction.

Solomon

The first problem we face is the long section on Solomon (11 chapters) where it would be very easy to get becalmed, especially in the extended descriptions of the building of the temple. Yet clearly these chapters are vital in establishing the values and perspectives of the book. My approach was to take the chapters as a whole and, following the dynamics of the narrative, establish the situation and detect seeds of decline which led to the Exile. This involved studying why the grandeur and gifts of Solomon failed to prevent his decline, the Bible's classic tragic character. The sermon title 'Half-hearted commitment' already suggests the main thrust of the application: Solomon, like the church in Laodicea (Revelation 3.16), was 'neither hot nor cold' and stands as a warning to all who flirt with God.

The Schism

This leads naturally on to the next stage of the story and how the kingdom was torn in two, the rump in Judah continuing under Rehoboam and the northern ten tribes or 'Israel' seized by Jeroboam, mentioned in 11.28 as 'a man of standing' and placed in charge of a northern workforce by Solomon. The title again suggests the thrust of the message. Rehoboam broke the first commandment (see 14.22-24) and effectively crushed the worship of Yahweh in Judah. Jeroboam broke the second commandment and introduced a syncretistic worship of Yahweh represented by the golden calves in Bethel, itself a deliberate echo of the golden calf made by Aaron in Exodus 32. Both sprung from the bad example set by Solomon in his declining years (11.1-8) and both in varying forms are to dominate much of the subsequent history that led eventually to the exile.

The Prophets' Ministry

Already we have seen, especially in the story of the man of God and the old prophet (reference?), the significance of the prophetic word and its vital bearing on the fortunes of the kingdoms. This is why the next four sermons concentrated on the flood of prophetic activity particularly associated with Elijah and Elisha. After a series of brief notices of kings of Judah and Israel, one of the Bible's most majestic figures, Elijah, appears abruptly to bring the word of the Lord to Ahab. Four sermons out of ten might seem a large number but is justified by the flow of the story. Almost a third of the text from 1 Kings 17 to 2 Kings 13 focusses on the prophets' ministry. Within this long section a further selection has to be made.

chapter 18 is one of the Old Testament's great set piece narratives. It is a brilliantly told story which powerfully dramatizes the stark choice between Yahweh and Baal. It clears the fog and sharply defines the choice to be made now as well as then. Nowhere is the necessity to commit ourselves fully to one way of life or the other so clearly presented.

The reason for choosing the story of Naboth's vineyard is 1 Kings 21 was to illustrate the strong social and communal thrust of the prophetic message. If 'Yahweh is God' that has implications for lifestyle and attitudes to property which are clearly brought out in this story. Thus the two studies together give a clear insight into the nature and role of prophecy in ancient Israel as well as having clear applications for the present.

Rather than taking another Elijah story I decided to study Micaiah's vision in 1 Kings 18. This draws attention to the great flood of prophetic activity in Israel and Judah and the problem of distinguishing authentic and inauthentic prophecy. The sermon concentrated on seeing and hearing God and explored the establishment voice, the uncertain voice of Jehoshaphat and the authentic voice of Micaiah. All these studies are painting a picture of ways in which the genuine voice of God can be heard.

I selected the story of Naaman in 2 Kings 5 to represent the Elisha stories because it illustrates many of the important themes of the prophetic narratives. The relevance of the gospel to nations other than Israel, the relation of providence to human circumstances and the response to the grace of God are clearly brought out in a well constructed narrative with clever character sketches.

By now we have a clear understanding of the prophetic critique of the failure of God's people to live as the covenant community as well as numerous indications of how this could be put right. Meanwhile the rather depressing and uninspiring occupants of the royal thrones succeed each other with many fascinating asides and insights, and an especially interesting reign, that of Joash, in 2 Kings 11 and 12.

'Joash tries to put it right' focuses on a new king who begins well but ends disastrously, assassinated by his own officials. Details are filled out by the Chronicler in 2 Chronicles 24 but the outlines are clear enough here. Again, picking up hints both in these chapters and in the wider narrative we can see why Joash failed. Unlike the earlier reforms of Asa and the later, greater reforms of Josiah, for Joash there is merely a job to be done, money to be raised and fabric repaired. There is a strange lack of personal faith and neglect of the word of God.

Josiah and Hezekiah

Thus the rot continues until Israel is taken off to exile in Assyria and the grim prospect of a total exile inches nearer. Then to the throne of Judah comes a young man in whose qualities and administration, people seem to see again the great days of David. So sermons 8 and 9 are devoted to the great reforming kings, Hezekiah and Josiah. Of both it is said there never was a king like him before or after (2 Kings 18.5 and 23.25). This apparent contradiction is resolved when we see how the text emphasizes different ways in which this was so. Hezekiah stands up to the Philistine Goliath and Josiah undertakes

10

HOW SHALL WE BEGIN?

the most thorough-going reformation of Israel's life and worship. In the Hezekiah story I emphasized many deliberate links with the story of David and Goliath.[6] Both the scale and ultimate failure of Josiah's reformation is emphasized along with the way in which the exile was now seen to be inevitable.

The last sermon 'O come, O Come Immanuel' (preached, as it happened, at the beginning of Advent) spoke of the challenge of exile to Israel's faith. Linking the end of Kings with Matthew 1 highlighted God's providence at work in people and circumstances, steadily leading to Christ, the true King in whom all the failed hopes and broken promises would ultimately be fulfilled.

Two further points can usefully be noted. The first is that the success of a series of this kind depends on being on top of the material. A few sentences linking the various episodes and pointing to the wider scene helps the flow. I provided a handout with an outline of the kings of Judah and Israel which many people found helpful as reference material.

The second is that we must work hard at application which earths the sermons is contemporary experience. This will be well done insofar as the narrative and theological structure of the book is grasped. The book must live for the preacher, worked out not only in the study but in daily life. Only then will it live for others.

---

6   This is a reminder that Samuel/Kings form a continuous narrative on the rise and fall of the monarchy.

3
Half-hearted Commitment: Solomon (1 Kings 1–11)

In my youth, the announcement that we were to visit a museum was usually greeted with muffled groans. Museums were solemn, musty places with a strangely close and uninspiring atmosphere where exhibits from the past were stored and catalogued under glass cases. It was difficult, in these circumstances to see our ancestors as living, breathing human beings.

Many contemporary museums by contrast are vital and exciting places. If you visit the Yorvik Centre in York you will travel in a time-car to a lovingly reconstructed Viking village and experience its smells and sounds. In the ABC museum in the same city you can sift through and reconstruct centuries' old remains of the city's life. There you can become vividly aware of the people and events of the past and savour something of vanished days.

It is such an experience we are aiming at in our preaching of biblical narrative. We want to listen to the story of Solomon in order to let it speak to the present, and we need to ask certain questions of the text. Solomon is the supreme biblical example of tragedy in the classical sense—the story of someone with great gifts, unique privileges and almost unparalleled opportunities who not only squandered all these but left a legacy which tore his kingdom apart and led eventually to the exile of his people. The thrust of the sermon is indicated in the title 'Half-hearted commitment,' and this also suggests the enduring relevance of the story. I shall outline the pattern of the sermon and then comment on how it was constructed and what the implications are for preaching on this kind of narrative.

Outline of Sermon

Introduction. Something about the value and importance of Old Testament history would have to be said. This is not antiquarianism but an account of events in the real world where God is at work. This means we will focus on the acts of God, not simply humans, and we will be concerned how the individual stories fit into the Bible's plot line. We will ask two basic questions of the text:

1. *What made Solomon great?* The story gives us glimpses of a fabulous oriental world (see especially 1 Kings 4.20-34). This is 'Solomon in all his glory.' But we must explore this further.
   a) *God-given wisdom:* Solomon's accomplishments in the whole range of human life and activity is all built on wisdom which is a gift from God. But what does this magnificent monarch have to do with the

concerns of people in the pews?[7] The point is that wisdom is open to everyone—'If any of you lack wisdom he should ask God who gives generously' (James 1.5)—and the flow of the story shows what happened to Solomon when he turned his back on wisdom.

b) *Revelation from God:* Chapter 3 places Solomon in relation to the whole sweep of God's purposes. Moreover this is in the context of prayer and openness to God as well as the helplessness inseparable from falling asleep and dreaming.

c) *His building of the temple:* Here it is important not to get tangled in the architectural detail but again to discern the sweep of the narrative. It is significant that at a number of points there is deliberate allusion to the making of the Tent in the desert, as in the listing of materials used (8.48-50, compare Exodus 31.3-4). It is also necessary to comment on how this temple fits into the Bible's story line. Not only does it recall the Tent, but it also anticipates Ezekiel's rebuilt temple from which a life-giving stream flows into a desert. This in turn points to Christ 'pitching his tent among us' (John 1.14) and the heavenly city where there is no longer any need for a temple because God and the Lamb are there.

2. *Why did he fail?* We must pick up the hints in the text. But first, another question. Why, if David failed so spectacularly, was he a man 'after God's own heart?'[8] It may be that David's agonized repentance over Uriah and Bathsheba, nowhere paralleled in anything said of Solomon, is the key. In chapters 1 and 2 of 1 Kings Solomon appears as a rather ruthless political manipulator eliminating his rivals, for example, having Joab killed at the altar in the sanctuary.

Another clue comes in chapter 7. Chapter 6 has lovingly described the beauties of the temple and concludes—'He had spent seven years building it' (6.38). Chapter 7.1 continues: 'It took Solomon thirteen years, however, to complete the construction of his palace.'[9] We cannot build too much on silences but this silence is positively deafening. Why does the narrator feel it necessary to say that Solomon's own palace was given almost twice as much time as the temple? Is there a suggestion that the temple is being seen as his private chapel, an extension of his own domain? This makes it much easier to build other chapels for his foreign wives in honour of pagan deities.

---

7 The words of James Barr 'When the modern churchgoer is solemnly answered that he is in the same situation as the Prophet Moses, or Nicodemus or Cornelius, he ought to burst out laughing,' misses the point that it is precisely through paradigmatic individuals and events that God reveals his essential nature and purposes.

8 To argue, as some do, that the phrase 'after God's own heart' would be more accurately translated 'of God's own choice' hardly helps, because that still suggests God's approval.

9 The use of 'however' well brings out the force of the *waw* in the Hebrew text.

This impression is amplified by an increasing emphasis on luxury in chapters 9 and 10; gold is frequently mentioned (eg 9.11,14,28; 10.2,10,14,16,22). Indeed the lifestyle of Solomon is beginning to sound ominously like that of the kind of king Samuel warned would be the result of the people's demand for one (1 Samuel 8.11-17).

The main cause is Solomon's half-heartedness which is finally explicitly commented on in 11.4—although hinted at as far back as 3.3. Solomon here opens the floodgates to the syncretistic worship which was to be a feature of the later kingdoms and to lead directly to the exile. What Solomon tolerated, others followed, and the logical consequence was the policy of Ahab and Jezebel where pagan worship was no longer simply allowed but imposed.

Comments on Sermon

The above is not, of course, the sermon as it was actually preached although it follows the structure and leading ideas. Each of the points was illustrated and applied specifically to the congregation. I have omitted these as of local and occasional interest. The following points may be noted.

1. The didactic, interrogatory style seems to me to reflect the nature of the material in chapters 1-11 of 1 Kings. This is not, on the whole (except for perhaps parts of chapters 1 and 2) the kind of spell-binding narrative we have in, for example, 1 Kings 18 where Elijah confronts the prophets of Baal. Rather it reflects the kind of genre common in the Pentateuch where story is combined with lengthy description and some discourse. I think this echo of the Pentateuch is deliberate and indicates to us that the author wants to give to his work the same kind of authoritative status.
2. The interrogating of the text seems to be demanded by the nature of the story itself. It is true that chapter 11 comments explicitly on Solomon's story, but the kind of hints I have pointed out already invite us to question his motivation well before that. Thus, even at first reading, the theological statements of chapter 11 will not be a surprise and one of the pleasures of repeated rereadings will be to find these anticipations.
3. The flow of the story has been followed especially in the implied contrasts between, for example, the temple and Solomon's own house. This means that the sermon must be aware of and reflect those characteristics of narrative such as plot, characterization, style and setting mentioned earlier.
4. An important consideration when planning the sermon is how much of chapters 1-11 are going to be read out loud. There has not only to be a representative selection but also a few well-chosen words of introduction putting these in context. Reading narrative well is an indispensable part of bringing it alive.

4
The Lord Enthroned in Zion (2 Kings 18 and 19)

Most people enjoy a good adventure story full of tight corners and nail-biting incidents. It is exciting to read or watch the kind of episode where the heroine is trapped in an underground cellar where the water is rising and the hero has only moments to reach and rescue her. The story we now look at, told in 2 Kings 18 and 19, has just such a tension and a compelling power. This is a very different kind of writing from the leisurely narrative about Solomon.

Setting the Scene
At the beginning of the sermon it will be necessary to say something about the setting and the characters. Internally both northern and southern kingdoms had declined with weak kings and ineffective policies. In the north the end was reached in 721 BC when the Assyrians captured Samaria and deported the ten tribes to exile (17.3-6). The formidable Assyrian war machine was now menacing the tiny kingdom of Judah and it seemed only a matter of time before it too would go the way of the North.

Just at that moment there came to the throne of Judah a young man who seemed to bring an echo of the golden days of David. Hezekiah did much to undo the evils of his predecessors. We have a concise summary in 18.3-8 of the ways in which he stood out: his cultic reforms; his personal faith; his obedience to the Torah and his political and military initiatives. However, the emphasis of the narrator is on the struggle with Assyria and the situation of extreme danger to which this leads. Yet it is also important to emphasize that this is not primarily Hezekiah's story; it is God's story and as such part of the total plot line of the Bible. With this in mind it would be useful to take a small section of the narrative, Hezekiah's prayer (19.14-19) and use this as a lens through which to examine the whole story. This will enable us to be faithful to the flow of the story itself as well as the wider narrative of which it is part. So what is this prayer about?

Hezekiah's Prayer
Firstly, it is based on who God is. The fundamental question is not 'does God answer prayer?' but 'which God are we praying to?' The whole strategy of the Assyrian king Sennacherib was based on the belief that he was dealing with another local godlet. That can be seen in his boast in 18.33-35— 'Where are the gods of Hamath and Arpad? Where are the gods of Sepharvaim, Hena and Ivah? Have they rescued Samaria from my hand?'

Across the centuries we can hear the mocking sarcasm. That arrogance and further shaking of the mailed fist is seen in the whole incident of which that boast is part. Sennacherib is vigorously attacking Lachish, Judah's second city in the Judaean highlands, and sends an impressive embassy of the top brass to intimidate rather than negotiate with Hezekiah. The little phrase in v18 'they called for the king' has behind it all the swaggering arrogance of the so far unchallenged bullies.

Imaginative Reconstruction

This is one place where an imaginative reconstruction of what lies behind the laconic words is helpful. We can picture the baking sun, the crowds of panic-filled faces on the walls, the laughter and ribald arrogance of the Assyrians. We can imagine the deadly hush and the endless suspense as we wait for Hezekiah to appear. Will he come in his royal robes, will he wear armour, will he perhaps come as a penitent in sackcloth? If this were a film we could imagine now the camera playing on the city gate and the tension reaching breaking point as it creaks slowly open and we wait for the king to appear. Then a stunning move; it is not Hezekiah at all—no, it is his officials. If Sennacherib is going to negotiate with underlings so will Hezekiah. We can see how this man is a David. Do we not hear echoes of another story and another confrontation with another Goliath? 'You come to me with a sword and a spear but I come to you in the name of the Lord of hosts, the God of the armies of Israel, whom you have defied.'

Yet it all seems crazy. Sennacherib has history, politics and common sense on his side. Syria and Israel have been conquered and humiliated. In the interim between this embassy and the letter which prompts the prayer Lachish had fallen after a terrible siege.[10] The letter, whose substance is given in 19.10-13, repeats the boast, outlines the evidence for the Assyrian confidence and warns against 'the god you depend on.' This all gives a terrible urgency to Hezekiah's prayer and is the indispensable background for appreciating just how much all depends on God being who Hezekiah claimed he was.

Thus Hezekiah prays to the God of the Exodus, encapsulated in the phrase 'O Lord, God of Israel, enthroned between the cherubim.' This is the God who appointed the place he would meet with the people and indeed live among them.[11] This emphasis on the mercy seat shows that the Exodus was not simply an incidental action of God but a revelation of his innermost char-

---

10 Vivid bas-reliefs of the siege of Lachish were discovered on the walls of the main room of Sennacherib's principal palace in Nineveh. It is difficult to account for the lavish portrayal of the capture of an obscure town in a remote petty kingdom other than as propaganda to disguise the failure to take Jerusalem.

11 The phrases used here, while not a complete description of the Exodus, are the kind of expressions which regularly point to that event.

acter as a God who comes down to rescue and live among his people. Assyrian sculptures and bas-reliefs are full of pictures of vanquished monarchs kneeling before the Great King of Assyria; here Hezekiah is on his knees but it is before the king, the Lord of Hosts.

Secondly, Hezekiah's prayer is based on what God does. Just as the prayer looks back at the message of Sennacherib so it anticipates the message of Isaiah in 19.18-34. He prays to the God of Psalm 121 who 'made heaven and earth.' This is reinforced by the words of Isaiah which turn the boasts of the Assyrians against them.[12]

Moreover Hezekiah does not base his prayer on personal grounds such as 'I have been a good king, I deserve some favourable consideration.' Rather he bases his hopes on God's grace. In this he shows real vision. Vision is not seeing what is not there, it is seeing everything that is there. He does not deny the realities: 'It is true Lord, that the Assyrian kings have laid waste these nations and their lands' (19.17). But he sees beyond that to a greater reality. Now the vaunting power of Assyria seems to have diminished sadly as if we were looking at it through the wrong end of a telescope. The fearsome hordes dwindle to toy soldiers, the voices of the Assyrian top brass sound like a childish squeak as another voice speaks. This is the voice that said 'Let there be light,' the voice that split open the Red Sea, the voice that now says: 'Because you rage against me and your insolence has reached my ears, I will put my hook in your nose and my bit in your mouth, and I will make you return by the way you came' (19.28). As Isaiah 40.15 says, 'All the nations are like a drop in a bucket.'

Thirdly, it is based on God's honour. This prayer is missionary and outward-looking in its emphasis—'that all kingdoms on earth may know that you alone, O Lord, are God' (19.19). Something is about to happen because God will defend the city for his own sake and to honour his promise to David.

What Happened Next?

We have three sources of information. Sennacherib's version of events emphasizes the capture of forty six cities of Judah and draws a veil over his failure to capture Jerusalem. Some centuries later the Greek historian Herodotus said that a bubonic plague raged through the Assyrian camp decimating the army. Given the insanitary conditions of ancient warfare that seems a possible explanation. The biblical author sees it as a direct action of the Lord: 'That night the angel of the Lord sent out and put to death a hundred and eighty-five thousand men in the Assyrian camp' (19.35). This is yet another echo of the Exodus story (Exodus 14.19–20) where the angel of the

---

12 Sargon, Sennacherib's father in his annals uses phrases such as 'I passed through high mountains covered with trees, whose passes are fearful;' 'I set up my camp on the mountain' which are echoed in Isaiah's words in 2 Kings 19.22ff.

Lord comes between the armies of Israel and Egypt. This is the event interpreted by the prophetic word.

Perhaps this event is also echoed in Psalm 48 where the kings fled in terror and the psalmist urges the faithful to 'Walk about Zion, go round her, count her towers, consider well her ramparts, view her citadels, that you may tell of them to the next generation' (vv 12,13). Zion is still there; God has defended her.

General Comments

The sermon was constructed around four main principles

1. An attempt was made to bring out the drama and tension of the story by focussing on some of the implied highlights of the plot. This was not done by simply retelling the story but by drawing out the feelings and emotions lying under the surface of the text.
2. Emphasis was laid on the place of this story in the Bible's plot line. This was shown by the frequent references to the Exodus as well as to David. Indeed, the great issue is faithfulness to and trust in the Lord who made the covenant with Moses and later with David. There is a massive irony in the word of the Assyrian commander, 'Choose life and not death' (18.31) after he had promised them a land of wine and honey. This is exactly the promise that the Lord made in Deuteronomy and urges the people 'to choose life' (Deuteronomy 30.19). So at this moment of crisis the question of the reliability of the God of Israel is not abstract theology but very literally a matter of life and death.
3. Similarly we have a theology of prayer in this story. As we have seen, the phrases used in the prayer with their echoes of the Psalms are not simply pious expressions they relate prayer to the heart of Israel's faith in the God of creation and history. Once again this is an illustration of the very practical nature of biblical theology and its relevance to the great issues of life and death.
4. The sermon was originally preached at the beginning of Advent and was a useful reminder that the whole Bible bears witness to the truths fully revealed in the coming of Christ. For here we have the very heart of the biblical gospel—a God who visits and redeems his people.

5
Where Do We Go From Here?

The whole thrust of the booklet has been to be practical as well as theological and indeed to show that good practise arises from sound theology. The question that many who have read this far will be asking is 'What happens now?' Some may agree that this is a good idea and yet be rather nervous about tackling long stretches of narrative themselves. In this final chapter some suggestions will be offered, some conclusions drawn and further reading outlined.

Getting Down to the Task

As noted earlier, there is no substitute for reading and rereading the texts. Only thus will the flow of the books and their distinctive emphases be clearly fixed in our minds. This will also, incidentally, have the important effect of helping to shape our minds to think biblically which is to think with the mind of Christ. It is also useful to read different translations, especially when coming to detailed work on individual passages.[13] A further useful practise is to listen to tapes of the relevant biblical books. Car journeys, for example, can be opportunities to listen to Scripture.

If you find it daunting to plan a series on such a large block of material as 1 and 2 Kings there are various ways of beginning. One way is to take a short book such as Ruth or Jonah and preach and teach the essence of them in three or four sermons or talks. A further useful discipline would be to try to teach the essence of the book in one sermon.

Another way to begin this kind of preaching is to tackle a well-defined section of a larger narrative block, such as the Joseph story (Genesis 37-50). This has a good, strong flowing narrative with plenty of suspense and subtle characterization. It also has a strong theological current which surfaces explicitly in 50.20—'You intended to harm me, but God intended it for good.'[14] In 1 and 2 Kings, the ministry of Elijah and Elisha (1 Kings 17—2 Kings 13) could be tackled, or the reforming kings Hezekiah and Josiah (2 Kings 17-23).

Background Reading

While reading of the primary texts is vital, it is necessary to have a good background knowledge to help us to interpret the text faithfully. Some grasp

---

1 3 See R T France and P Jenson, *Translating the Bible* (Grove Biblical Series No 3)
14 Genesis 50.20 is a rich text which, among other things, recalls the evil thoughts and planning of Noah's contemporaries (Genesis 6.5). It is one of the classic texts which highlight both God's sovereignty and human responsibility.

of historical background is essential; much of this may be given in commentaries. Although now rather dated, J Bright's, *History of Israel* (OTL, revised edition, 1981) reads well and gives a good sense of the flow of events.

However, for preachers and teachers the basic requirement is a good library of commentaries.

In Grove's *Biblical Studies Bulletin* Vol 3, March 1997, Iain Provan has provided a useful summary of commentaries on Kings which everyone interested in these books should be aware of. If busy ministers are looking for one comprehensive commentary which is accurate, up to date and a real help in preaching then I would recommend Provan's own.[15] Here at last is the commentary preachers and teachers of the books of Kings have been waiting for. The text is treated as a whole as a coherent narrative and there is a fine introduction setting out clearly the kind of writing Kings is.

Some Practical Issues

Three matters of a practical nature need to be considered. Firstly, the kind of preaching advocated in this booklet has clear implications for the minister's time and thus consequences for the whole pattern of ministry. Diligent work on text and commentaries and a serious engagement with contemporary issues and application are time consuming and need a lot of discipline. Two comments may be helpful.

All ministers must work out their own priorities. Some may think that this kind of preaching implies spending every morning at the desk which may have been possible in past generations but not any longer. It probably never was possible to have that pattern, but some mornings at least ought to be possible. These must be timetabled and only abandoned for emergencies and the temptation to potter must be resisted. It is also valuable to try to set aside at least a day a month for more extended reading and study.

The other point is that this booklet is written with the conviction that the flock needs to be fed and cared for and that the Word of God is the main way of doing this. Failure to give time to this is like feeding our family or guests on an endless diet of fast food snacks. Time spent in preparation and prayer is not a diversion from pastoral work, it is the heart of pastoral work.

Secondly, the task of preaching on narrative or any other kind of biblical literature is to send people back to the Bible with renewed enthusiasm. It is Scripture, not our words about it, which is life-giving. This is why we need to work hard at preaching in order to make the text as accessible as possible to people. A vital part of any such attempt is a clear and articulate reading of the text. Often in long narrative stretches there will have to be a careful se-

---

15 I Provan, *1 and 2 Kings* (NIBC, Hendrickson, 1995). See also his *1 and 2 Kings* in the OT Guide Series (Sheffield Academic Press, 1997).

lection and brief explanatory introductions. In churches with many capable readers these brief remarks could be left to them. In other circumstances, the minister may well want to write these down for the readers. It is important that people realize that the public reading of Scripture is a vital ministry and that help is given in this where necessary.

Thirdly, preaching on biblical narrative will help congregations in all kinds of ways. It will give a sense of the coherence of the whole Bible's story line and thus of the integrity of the gospel. It will 'earth' the most doctrinal passages by showing how God's people have had to work out their faith in changing circumstances. It will continue to expand their horizons and help them to see God at work in the world.

The Value of the Task

Three basic principles underlie what has been said.

This booklet has been written in the conviction that the whole Bible is valuable and relevant. In terms of preaching there is no such thing as a 'no go area.' This means that the Old Testament is not simply to be read and preached on in terms of a few 'purple passages' such as 1 Kings 18, Isaiah 53 and Psalm 23, but to be studied as a whole. It is not simply an introduction to the gospel; it is part of the gospel and indispensable for understanding the Bible's plot line.

In Old Testament narrative that relevance is seen on at least three levels. Ancient Israel was a political entity, a nation (or two nations), and thus there is a message to the national and international scene, principles of behaviour and a theology of history. But ancient Israel was also the people of God and thus there is a message to the church. Thirdly there is a message to individuals about their personal walk with God and the choices they make. All these interpenetrate and some passages are more directly relevant on one level than on the other. This realization will help us to avoid faulty exegesis and the kind of moralizing preaching identified in chapter 1 as one of the main pitfalls of preaching from Old Testament narrative.

In the second place, this kind of study and preaching will force us to listen carefully to the text and take it with full imaginative seriousness. In the first place that will mean our own theological grid will be challenged by the passage rather than the other way round. I have already argued in chapter 1 that these are related to the basic issues of plot, characterization, setting, style and world-view as well as to the overall place of the passage in the whole plot of the Bible. This will further mean that while we may well believe that the sacrifices in Leviticus and the suffering servant in Isaiah find their unique and ultimate fulfilment in Christ (as this writer certainly does), we will not avoid the effort of trying to understand the context in which the passages were written.

21

It will also mean that our hearts and personalities will be involved as well as our minds. We will understand something of what it was to be God's people in ancient times. We shall travel there so that we can travel back and demonstrate the continuing relevance of their story. This imagination must be disciplined and creative so that we will both be faithful to the text and imaginative in our application of it to the contemporary world.

Finally, this kind of preaching will have a profound effect on our whole attitude to mission and even apologetics. If the story is the message, then our presentation of the gospel will be anchored to the Bible's coherent plot. This will save us from the kind of over-hasty application of, for example, the story of David and Goliath already mentioned. It will also save us from hasty decisions on the interpretation of such stories as Joshua's slaughter of the Canaanites. This does not mean that every time we share the gospel that we will have to give a summary of the whole Bible story. It does mean that we will need to fit what we say into that and be able to handle it. We live increasingly in a day when people scarcely even know that the Bible has two Testaments. In these circumstances simply quoting a text about Jesus and using such words as redemption are likely to be met with blank looks. An increasingly helpful model is that of Paul in Acts 17 where, speaking to the philosophers in Athens, he goes through the great biblical doctrines of creation, providence and resurrection showing how these culminate in Christ.

That underlines a second important consideration which has been implicit in all that has been said. The great truths of creation, providence, salvation history, wisdom, and so on, are assumed in the New Testament because they are covered in such detail in the Old Testament. Many of these are embodied in narrative and must be understood if we are to appreciate the New Testament adequately. The way the New Testament uses the Old Testament is another fascinating study in itself and cannot be explored here.

'Were not our hearts burning within us while he talked with us on the road and opened the Scriptures to us?' (Luke 24.32). That is our aim in all our listening to and teaching of the Bible. Opening the Scriptures leads to enlightened minds and burning hearts and sets us on the road again with the message that the Lord has risen.

Bibliography

I would like to emphasize again that there is no substitute for repeated readings of the biblical text. Secondly, good commentaries, like some of those mentioned in chapter 6 are indispensable. The following are a selection of relevant books; mention of a book does not necessarily imply agreement with its stance.

Alter, Robert, *The Art of Biblical Narrative* (New York: Basic Books, 1981). Still one of the best studies of biblical literature. See also his *The World of Biblical Literature* (SPCK, 1992)

Bar-Efrat, Shimon, *Narrative Art in the Bible* (Sheffield Academic Press, 1989). Originally written in Hebrew and a useful guide to modern Jewish perspectives.

Berlin, Adele, *Poetics and Interpretation of Biblical Narrative* (Indiana: Eisenbrauns, 1984). One of the most accessible surveys of literary criticism.

Coggins, Richard, *Introducing the Old Testament* (OUP, 1990). A useful guide to different approaches to the OT—see especially chapter 8.

Greidanus, Sidney, *The Modern Preacher and the Ancient Text* (IVP, 1988). A comprehensive guide to preaching and literary forms.

Gunn, David M and Fewell, Danna Nolan, *Narrative in the Hebrew Bible* (OUP, 1993). A survey of current theories with examples.

Hauerwas, Stanley and Jones, L Gregory, *Why Narrative?* (Eerdmans, 1989). A cluster of views on story and theology.

Kort, Wesley A, *Story, Text and Scripture* (Pennsylvania UP, 1988). A study of the relationship between narrative and theology.